Written by Cathy Varvaris and Jane L. Fryar

Unless otherwise indicated, all Scripture quotations are taken from the Holy Bible, New Living Translation, copyright © 1996. Used by permission of Tyndale House Publishers, Inc., Wheaton, Illinois 60189. All rights reserved.

Copyright © 2003 by Christian Teachers Aid, 1625 Larkin Williams Rd., Fenton, MO 63026-2404.

All rights reserved. No part of this publication may be reproduced, stored in a retrieval system, or transmitted, in any form or by any means, electronic, mechanical, photocopying, recording, or otherwise, without the prior written permission of Christian Teachers Aid.

ISBN 0-9718985-2-9
Printed in the United States of America

Dear—————————————————,

Your name goes in here! We don't know it yet, but Jesus did before you were even born! Wow!

Who is your best friend? How do you talk to your best friend? Do you ever e-mail or instant message with your best friend? (In case you don't think you have a best friend, don't forget about Jesus! He is ready and able to be your best friend every day of your life, starting now!)

Jesus <u>is</u> the best friend you could ever have, and each page of this journal gives you suggestions for things to talk about with him. Each page has a Bible verse and shows you how to write a prayer about something in that verse. When you're finished, you might want to read your prayer aloud, just as if you were talking to Jesus. But if you don't, that's okay, because prayer with Jesus is like instant messaging: he hears it as soon as you send it, whether it's read aloud or not.

And don't forget that Jesus loves you very much and is always listening when you talk (or write) to him. In fact, he's glad to listen to you! So have fun with this journal and have fun enjoying Jesus as your best friend!

Using your prayer journal

 Be free when you write to Jesus! He knows and loves you, so there's no reason to try to hide your mistakes or your sins.

Praise. Sometimes when we pray, we remember how great God is. We tell him about that in words of praise. Praise and thanks go together so closely, you may not be able to tell them apart. Here's one example of a prayer praise:

Lord, you are so good, so ready to forgive, so full of unfailing love for all who ask your aid. (Psalm 86:5)

Repent. When we start to praise God for how good he is, we remember that we are NOT always good. We remember the times we have disobeyed God by failing to show love for him or for others around us. We feel ashamed and guilty. We may even feel afraid that God will punish us. But we also need to remember that Jesus took our punishment for us. He let himself be nailed onto a wooden cross to suffer the punishment we deserve. Now God forgives every one of our sins. We are pure and clean in God's sight. Here's a Bible verse about that:

I confessed all my sins to you ... and stopped trying to hide them. I said to myself, "I will confess my rebellion to the Lord." And you forgave me! All my guilt is gone. (Psalm 32:5)

Remember, Jesus is God. The heavenly Father is God. And, the Holy Spirit is God. Remember, too, that you can pray to God, the Father, the Son, or the Holy Spirit. Each part of God wants to hear and answer your prayers.

Learn to "P.R.A.Y." The meaning behind each letter in "pray" will help you when you're stuck! "P" stands for praise. "R" stands for repent. "A" stands for ask. "Y" stands for yield.

Ask. When we're in trouble, Jesus wants us to come to him. He will always hear and help us. Sometimes when we ask for something, he says "Yes!" right away. Sometimes he says, "I have something better in mind." Even if we don't see his answers or something bad happens, we can trust Jesus to do what's best for us. After all, he died for us! Here is a Bible verse about that:

> **Since God did not spare even his own Son, but gave him up for us all, won't God, who gave us Christ, also give us everything else? (Romans 8:32)**

Yield. Yield means to let someone else have his way. God gives us courage to ask Jesus to have his way when we pray.. Yielding means we trust Jesus will answer our prayers in the way that is best for us. It means we know he is taking good care of us, no matter what happens. More and more, we want to love, trust, and obey him. Here is a Bible verse about that:

> **May [God's] will be done here on earth, just as it is in heaven. (Matthew 6:10)**

DAY 1

> I will answer them before they even call me. ...I will go ahead and answer their prayers!
> — Isaiah 65:24

Even before you pray, Jesus has answered your prayers.
So why do we pray? We pray for lots of reasons.
Here's one: Just like you run to tell your mom or dad or friends about important things that happen, you can run to tell Jesus everything that's on your heart. Below, write to tell him about something exciting that happened today. Be sure to include a big "P" from the P.R.A.Y. kind of prayer—Praise!

DAY 2

> Don't worry about anything; instead, pray about everything. Tell God what you need, and thank him for all he has done.
> — Philippians 4:6

Even though Jesus knows what we need, he wants us to tell him what worries us and to let him take care of our problems. Telling Jesus about our worries is good for us because it reminds us that he knows what we need and will take care of us.

Write to tell Jesus about what worries you today. Ask him to help you stop worrying. As you write, try using the "Y" from the P.R.A.Y. kind of prayer—Yield!

DAY 3

> LORD! You have made the heavens and earth by your great power. Nothing is too hard for you!
> — Jeremiah 32:17

God is awesome! He created everything you see—and many things you can't see. He made the stars in the skies and the bugs on the ground. Some people think God is too busy to bother with our little problems. But our God is mighty <u>and</u> loving. No problem is too small or too hard for him. Write about a problem that you thought was too big for God to fix. Or write about a problem you thought was too small. Think about the "A" from the P.R.A.Y. kind of prayer.

DAY 4

> I wait quietly before God, for my salvation comes from him.
> — Psalm 62:1

We sin every day. We know what's right, but we do what's wrong. God gives us many chances to show love, but we act selfishly instead. What then? The Bible says, "God's kindness leads us to repentance" (Romans 2:4). God helps us see our sins. He helps us to feel sorry for them and to want to stop doing them. He forgives us—washing away our sin because of what Jesus did for us. On the lines below, confess your sins; tell God what you've done. Ask him to forgive you and help you obey him.

DAY 5

> Afterward [Jesus] went up into the hills by himself to pray. Night fell while he was there alone.
> — Matthew 14:23

No one has ever been closer to God than Jesus, but Jesus still took time to be alone with God, his heavenly Father. God wants to talk with you every day. Do you have a special place where you like to be alone with him? A place where you like to pray? Describe that place. Then write to praise God for letting you get close to him and talk to him. Use the "P" from the P.R.A.Y. kind of prayer.

DAY 6

> Ask me and I will tell you some remarkable secrets about what is going to happen here.
> — Jeremiah 33:3

Have you ever wanted to ask God a question? About why he created a giraffe, or what he wants you to be when you grow up? Ask him! He will help you find answers to your questions. Use this page to write one or more important questions. Then ask God to help you find the answers— maybe in the Bible; maybe from one of your parents or teachers or pastor; or maybe as you live your life day by day.

DAY 7

> And we can be confident that [Jesus] will listen to us whenever we ask him for anything in line with his will.
> —1 John 5:14

When we are <u>confident,</u> we believe Jesus hears our prayers. It doesn't matter how many times you have disobeyed him or how long it's been since you last prayed. Jesus promised to always hear our prayers! You don't have to wait in line to talk to him or leave a message on his answering machine because he's not home. Jesus is ready and waiting to hear you. In the space below, tell Jesus how you feel, knowing that he's listening no matter what.

DAY 8

> Wait patiently for the LORD. Be brave and courageous. Yes, wait patiently for the Lord.
> — Psalm 27:14

Does God answer every prayer? Yes! Sometimes exactly as you ask; sometimes even better! But sometimes, it seems as if his answer is taking a long time or isn't the best answer. In those times, remember that God gave Jesus to die for you and will always do what's best for you. What have you been praying about? How do you think God is answering your prayer? Talk to him about that as you write. (Before you write, review the "Y" part of a P.R.A.Y. prayer.)

DAY 9

> One day Jesus told his disciples a story ... to show them that they must never give up.
> — Luke 18:1

Since we know that Jesus always answers our prayers, why do we need to keep praying? For one reason, it reminds us from day to day or even minute to minute that we can trust God to handle our problems and that we don't need to worry. Today, write to tell God how it feels to wait a long time for an answer to a prayer.

DAY 10

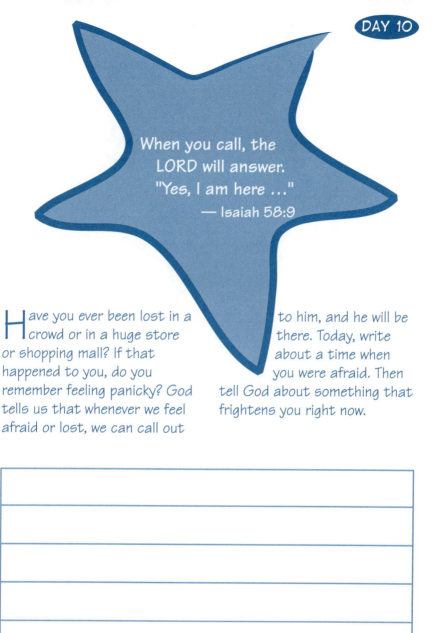

When you call, the LORD will answer. "Yes, I am here ..."
— Isaiah 58:9

Have you ever been lost in a crowd or in a huge store or shopping mall? If that happened to you, do you remember feeling panicky? God tells us that whenever we feel afraid or lost, we can call out to him, and he will be there. Today, write about a time when you were afraid. Then tell God about something that frightens you right now.

DAY 11

> Confess your sins to each other and pray ... The earnest prayer of a righteous person has great power and wonderful results.
> — James 5:16

Have you ever wanted to hide because you had done something wrong? When we sin, God wants us to repent—to ask for his forgiveness. Because Jesus died for our sins in our place on the cross, we don't have to hide anymore. We can tell God we are sorry and he always forgives us for Jesus' sake. Then we can ask those we've hurt for forgiveness, and trust God to heal our relationships with them. Write a prayer, asking God to forgive you for the things you've done wrong. (Remember that repentance is the second part of the P.R.A.Y. kind of prayer.)

DAY 12

> When you are praying, first forgive anyone you are holding a grudge against …
> — Mark 11:25

Sometimes when we are praying, we remember the times other people have hurt us. It isn't always easy to forgive them or drop the grudge we're holding against them. But God wants us to forgive. Hating others and wanting to get even with them hurts us. It makes our hearts hard and bitter. God doesn't want that for us! Is there someone you need to forgive? Ask Jesus to help you remember how much love and forgiveness he has shown you. Then ask him to help you love others the same way and forgive them the way he forgives you.

DAY 13

> Always be joyful...
> No matter what happens, be thankful, for this is God's will for you who belong to Christ Jesus.
> — 1 Thessalonians 5:16-18

When you've had a great day, it's easy to be thankful. This passage reminds us to be thankful all the time! Even on the worst day we can thank God for something. Since you belong to Jesus, you can have a thankful attitude no matter what. On the lines below, tell Jesus ten things you are thankful for today.

DAY 14

> Trust me in all your times of trouble, and I will rescue you, and you will give me glory.
> — Psalm 50:15

When we need to choose between right and wrong, Jesus invites us to call on him. He promises to help us make the right choice. Making the right choice doesn't always please our friends, but it does always please Jesus. On these lines, tell about a decision you need to make and ask Jesus to help you decide what to do.

DAY 15

> God ... will supply all your needs from his glorious riches, which have been given to us in Christ Jesus.
> — Philippians 4:19

Do you find yourself saying, "I need this video game" or "I need that new shirt"? Do you really need it, or do you just want it? As you grow up, you are learning that what you want and what you need are not always the same thing. God promises to give us everything we need. But we may not always get everything we want. In the space below, thank Jesus for some of the needs and some of the wants he has meant for you.

DAY 16

> When you call, the LORD will answer. "Yes, I am here..."
> — Isaiah 58:9

Sometimes problems seem so big we can't see any way around them. We don't even know how to ask God to help us. We feel like we're lost in a dark forest, and we don't know which way to turn. The Bible promises that when we are confused and distressed, the Holy Spirit is already praying for us. Tell the Holy Spirit how you feel, knowing that he loves you so much he is always praying for you.

DAY 17

> The LORD is my strength, my shield from every danger. I trust in him with all my heart ... I burst out in songs of thanksgiving.
> — Psalm 28:7

Think of a time you had to do something you were afraid to do. Maybe it was jumping into the deep end of the pool. Or maybe you needed to tell your mom about getting into trouble in school. God wants to give you the strength you need. He is always there to help you face any situation. In the space below, tell about a time that knowing God was with you helped you do something hard. Thank him for being there.

DAY 18

> Devote yourselves to prayer with an alert mind and a thankful heart.
> — Colossians 4:2

Sometimes when we know we need Jesus, we wonder if he's really there. Later we realize he was, even though we didn't feel close to him at the time. When we pray "with an alert mind and a thankful heart," we are watching to see how Jesus is working. We keep looking for his answers, and we thank him for keeping his promises. When have you seen God answer one of your prayers? Write about it in the space below, with thanks.

DAY 19

> Seek the LORD while you can find him. Call on him now while he is near.
> — Isaiah 55:6

Some people think God is like Santa Claus. To these people, prayer becomes asking him greedily for lots of goodies. Prayer isn't like that! This passage tells us that when we pray, we seek the Giver more than his gifts!

What we need most is Jesus' love and forgiveness. Knowing that we have those, we ask him to give us other things that would be best for us. Have you ever asked a parent for advice? Often, prayer is asking God for advice.

DAY 20

> Let us hold tightly to the hope we say we have, for God can be trusted to keep his promise.
> — Hebrews 10:23

Who can you count on? Your mom? Dad? A brother or sister? A good friend? Sometimes, the people we love the most let us down. They forget a promise or disappoint us in some other way. But our Savior is different. He always does what he has said. If you have trouble believing that, you can ask Jesus to give you more faith. Today, write about a lost hope. What made you feel better? Praise Jesus for being able and willing to help.

DAY 21

> The LORD is God! He made us, and we are his. We are his people, the sheep of his pasture.
> — Psalm 100:3

A shepherd spends all day and night with the sheep. The shepherd finds fresh food and water for them and protects them from wolves. Sheep aren't very smart. Sometimes one will wander off and get lost. Then the shepherd has to look for it. The sheep know their shepherd's voice and only follow him. How is Jesus like a good shepherd? (Read John 10:1-18 to learn more about this.) Tell Jesus why you're glad to be one of his sheep.

DAY 22

> I love the LORD because he hears and answers my prayers. Because he bends down and listens, I will pray as long as I have breath!
> — Psalm 116:1-2

When a baby cries, its mom picks it up to find out what it needs. Mom will see if it needs clean diapers, milk to drink, burping, or just comfort. The baby learns that when it needs something it just needs to cry. God is a little like that. Because God always hears and answers our prayers, we learn to call to him every day. Cry out to God today with your needs. Listen for his voice. Make a list of his answers that you can thank him for today.

DAY 23

> O LORD my God, I cried out to you for help, and you restored my health.
> — Psalm 30:2

People often ask God to make them well after nothing else has worked. But God wants us to call on him first when we need healing. God uses doctors, nurses, medicine, and other treatments to help us. Sometimes he heals us without any medical treatment. We can pray before we go to the doctor and while we're there. Tell God about people in your life who need healing. Use the "A" of the P.R.A.Y. kind of prayer—asking him to help these people.

DAY 24

> What is faith? It is the confident assurance that what we hope for is going to happen. It is the evidence of things we cannot yet see.
> — Hebrews 11:1

Most people use the word "hope" in the same way they use the word "wish." They might say, for example, "I hope it doesn't rain on our ballgame." But in the Bible, hope is not an empty wish. We can count on the "hope" Jesus gives. We can have faith that he will do what he says he will do. That's what "confident assurance" means. Write to Jesus about the promises he's made to you in the Bible to give you hope.

DAY 25

> I urge you to pray for all people. As you make your requests, plead for God's mercy upon them, and give thanks.
> —1 Timothy 2:1

This verse reminds us to pray for others. This kind of praying is called "intercessory prayer." Earlier in this journal, we said that the Holy Spirit prays for us when we don't know what to ask God to do for us. The Holy Spirit "intercedes" for us, and we can "intercede" for others. Write to God about someone who doesn't know Jesus as the Savior. Ask God to show you how to tell that person about Jesus.

DAY 26

> Dear brothers and sisters, pray for us.
> — 1 Thessalonians 5:25

We can "intercede" or "pray for" those who don't know Jesus. But we can intercede for people with other needs, too- those who are lonely, hurt, in need of a job, or going on a trip. Whenever we see someone else with any kind of need, we can talk to God for them, asking his help and blessing. Think of three people and intercede for them today. Write in your journal what you've asked God to do.

THE END

> "For I know the plans I have for you," says the LORD. "They are plans for good and not for disaster, to give you a future and a hope."
> —Jeremiah 29:11-12

This prayer journal has come to an end. But this is just the beginning of your prayer life! Keep writing out your prayers to Jesus. When you re-read your prayer journals a month or year or 10 years later, you will see all the things Jesus has taught you and all the great things he has done for you. Your journals will become a history of your walk with Jesus Christ. Remember, Jesus always loves you.